Book Works

NATHAN COLEY:
Urban / W:

Book Works

BRAZIL:

Rio de Janeiro → Brasília → Manaus → Amazonas ●

USA:

Los Angeles → Death Valley → Las Vegas → Mojave Desert → Joshua Tree National Park ●

SCOTLAND:

Edinburgh → Rannoch Moor ●

NATHAN COLEY:
Urban / Wild ●

ndaward Is
Guadeloupe
Dominica
Martinique
St Lucia
St Vincent
Barbados
Grenada
Tobago
Port of Spain
Trinidad

icao
emstad
Maracay
CARACAS
alencia
Maturin
Orinoco

VENEZUELA

GUYANA
Georgetown
Paramaribo
SURINAM
FR GUIANA
Cayenne

GUIANA HIGHLANDS

Negro

Macapa
Mouths of the Amazon
Marajo I
Equa

AMAZON

Manaus
Santarem
Cameta
Belem
Sao Luis

Madeira

abrea
Humaita

Teresina
Fortaleza

Joao Pessoa
Campina Grande
Natal
RECIFE
Olinda
Maceio
Aracaju

Araguaia
Tocantins
São Francisco

B   R   A   Z   I   L

Guapore

LIVIA

MATO
GROSSO

Salvador

Paz

Sucre
Corumba

Goiania
Brasilia

BRAZILIAN HIGHLANDS

Paraguay

CHACO
PARAGUAY

Parana

Ribeirao Preto

BELO HORIZONTE
Vitoria

Juiz de Fora
RIO DE JANEIRO
Niteroi

GRAN

Salta

Corrientes
Asuncion

Campinas
Sorocaba
SAO PAULO
Santo Andre
Santos

Tropic of Capric

Curitiba

Uruguai

Porto Alegre

doba
mdoza
Parana
Santa Fe
URUGUAY
Pelotas

Rosario
Quilmes
La Plata
BUENOS AIRES
MONTEVIDEO

RGENTINA
Mar del Plata
Bahia Blanca

ATLANTIC OCEAN

OCEAN

Charlotte Sound

Kemano
Prince George

MOUNTAINS

Vancouver I

Victoria
SEATTLE

Vancouver

Edmonton

Calgary

Prin

Saska

Astoria
Portland
Salem

Tacoma

Spokane

Red

CASCADE

Butte
Helena
Three Forks

Bismarc

Snake R

Great Salt L

MIN

Oakland
SAN
FRANCISCO

Sacramento

Salt Lake City

Ogden

Platte R

Stockton

Fresno

DENVER

Colorado Springs

Li

Death
Valley

Pueblo

LOS ANGELES

Pasadena

Bakersfield

Mojave
Desert

Las Vegas

Albuquerque

UNITED

Wich

STA

SAN DIEGO

Joshua Tree
Nat'l Park

Tijuana

Brawley

Mexicali

Phoenix

Tucson

Amari

Wichita Falls

adalupe I

Sebastian Vizcaino B

Gulf of California

Ciudad Juarez

Fort Worth

Rio Grande

Hermosillo

San Antonio

Austin

Chihuahua

Laredo

Tropic of Cancer

Culiacan

Torreon

Monterrey

Durango

Saltillo

MEXICO

Aquasalientes

San Luis

Fair Isle

Westray · North Ronaldsay

ORKNEY Sanday

ISLANDS

Hoy Kirkwall

Scapa Flow

Pentland South Ronaldsay

Thurso Duncansby Hd

Cape Wrath John O'Groats

North *Minch* Wick

Butt of Lewis *Little Halibut Ba*

HEBRIDES Stornoway

LEWIS L Shin

L *Shin*

Ullapool Dornoch

North Uist Dingwall Elgin Banff Fraserburgh

Moray Firth Peterhead

Little Minch Inverness *Spey* *Buchar*

Portree *Deep*

SKYE Kyle of *L Ness* CAIRNGORM

Lochalsh *Caledonian Canal* MTS Aberdeen

South Uist Fort Augustus

Rhum Mallaig *Dee* Ballater GRAMPIAN MTS Stonehaven

Barra Fort William GRAMPIAN MTS

L Linnhe *Rannoch* Forfar Montrose

Coll *Moor* Arbroath

Tiree **SCOTLAND** Perth Dundee

MULL Oban *L Awe* Perth

Inveraray *L Lomond* *Fife Ness*

Firth of Lorn *L Fyne* Stirling

Colonsay Jura *Firth of Forth*

ISLAY Paisley Edinburgh

Glasgow Berwick-upon- *Farr*

Kilmarnock *Tweed* *Dee*

Arran I SOUTHERN UPLANDS

Malin Head Ayr Hawick

NORTH Dumfries PENNINE

Coleraine *CHANNEL* CHEVIOT

ondonderry Stranraer Wigtown HILLS

GAL MTS *Bann* Carlisle Newcastle South

NORTHERN *L Neagh* *Luce* *Solway Firth* LAKE Durham Sund

IRELAND *Bay* DISTRICT Stockton We

Donegal Belfast CUMBRIAN Darlington Mi

L Eane Portadown CHAIN *Tees*

Armagh ISLE OF MTS

Newcastle Downpatrick MAN Barrow Lancaster *Ouse*

Carrick Cavan Douglas Morecambe Bay Bradford LEED

Longford Dundalk Blackpool Burnley

Boyne Drogheda *IRISH SEA* Preston Blackburn

L Ree MANCHESTER Oldham Stockport *Mudders*

RE Dublin LIVERPOOL Oldham She

Dun Laoghaire ANGLESEY Birkenhead Stockport

Bray Bangor Chester Crewe

Caernarvon *Mersey*

BRAZIL:
Rio de Janeiro →
Brasília → Manaus →
Amazonas ●

The beach along the Ipanema and Leblon strip. One of the most democratic places in Rio, where rich and poor alike enjoy the beautiful sand and sea.

Posto 9 at Ipanema, known as the 'Cemetério dos Elefantes' because of the old hippies, leftists and artists who hang out there.

Rio de Janeiro's Favelas

Seventeen percent of the population of Rio lives in favelas. There are close to 550 in Rio alone, mostly located on former public land on the hillsides around the city. Perched above the beaches of Ipanema, Leblon and Copacabana, their inhabitants have some of the best views in Brazil. The favelas of Rio are possibly the only place in the world where the poor live above the rich.

Visiting Vila Canoas

'The first thing to say is that you should feel safe. There is no robbery of tourists in the favelas. Robbery is bad for the drug dealers. Don't be shy, you are welcome here, and the local people support your visit, I am very well known. It is okay to take photographs, but no video. No straight shots of people from the community — no photography where the main part of the image is a person. This is not allowed. Do you understand. But feel free to make photographs. As you will see, people here live in poverty not misery. Yes they don't have much, but in the last ten years there have been improvements, which I will show you.'

— Marcelos Armstrong, guide/community worker in the favelas of Vila Canoas (pop. 2,500) and Rocinha (pop. 160,000)

Drug dealers

'If you respect him, he respects you. If you don't, he kills you. So you should respect him. He wants to sell marijuana and cocaine from here, to people from here, but mainly to people from Rio who have the money. They come here only because it is safe. There is no robbery here. People see a certain positive aspect to the presence of the drug dealer here because first he is a famous powerful man from where they live, somehow representing a power and a voice of the favelas. He has made this place a safe area. There is no robbery here. He has money enough to put part of his money back to invest into the necessities of the favelas. He tries to work here in ways that the government doesn't. On the other hand, we have the police — representing the other end of security. The police come from elsewhere in Rio, coming here sometimes aggressively, arrogantly. Sometimes when they come they shoot first and ask questions later. Most people don't much like the police behaviour in Rocinha. They might accept or respect or even eventually like the drug dealer because he is one of them.'

— Marcelos Armstrong

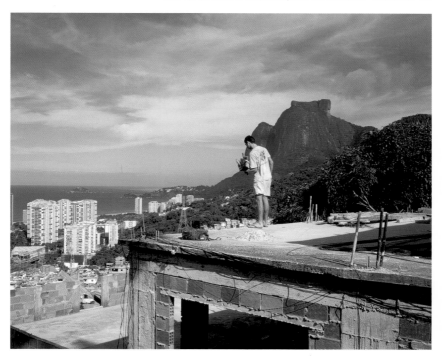

One of the most important recent developments in Rocinha has been the naming of its streets. With this, the inhabitants now have a postal address, which in turn allows them to formally register at the Town Hall. The paperwork of this may initially seem to have no affect on the living conditions of the favelas: however, with a recognised address comes the right to vote. The people of the favelas are for the first time on the radar of the city's politicians seeking election.

Brasília, Capital City of Brazil
Population: 2,052,100

....

1823
Idea of moving capital from Rio first mooted.

1956
Juscelino Kubitschek becomes President on the promise that he would build the city if he won the election.

After over 150 years of debate a site was identified in the barren sertão of the Goiás highlands region, one of Brazil's most isolated regions. 125km from the nearest rail link, 190km from the nearest airport, over 600km from the nearest paved road: the closest timber supply was 1,200km distance, the nearest source of good steel even further.

Rio's *Correio da Manha* newspaper coined the phrase 'The Limit of Insanity'.

Oscar Niemeyer, commissioned as architect, and Lucio Costa, as urban planner, start designing what will become the capital city of Brazil.

1960
Three years, one month and five days after the master plan was unveiled, 150,000 people arrived for the official inauguration ceremony. On that day only 150 first class hotel rooms had been completed for 5,000 visiting dignitaries.

1963
Simone de Beauvoir, visiting with Jean-Paul Sartre, described the city as 'elegant monotony'.

Growing population and ever expanding suburbs.

2004
Affluent city. Well-educated population. Administration centre to a country of over 170 million people.

Landmark of modernity, a monument that synthesises the union,
lightness and vastness of our horizons.

'I sought the curved and sensual line. The curve that I see in the Brazilian hills, in the body of a loved one, in the clouds, in the sky and in the ocean waves.'

— Oscar Niemeyer, Brasília architect

'The impression I get is that I have arrived on a different planet.'

— Yuri Gagarin, cosmonaut

Manaus

The capital of Amazonia, a tropical forest state covering around one and a half million square kilometres, thirty percent of the remaining forest of the world. The commercial and physical hub of the entire Amazonian region. Situated on the banks of the Rio Negro, six kilometres from the point where that river meets the Solimoes to form (as far as the Brazilians are concerned) the Rio Amazonas. It takes six days to sail by boat down stream to Belém at the mouth of the Amazon on the Atlantic Ocean and eight days up river to Colombia.

With its Parisian-style avenues and Italian piazzas much of the city's appearance is due to the rubber boom of the 1890s, when Manaus supplied much of Europe and America with raw materials for pneumatic tyres. In 1899 it was the first Brazilian city to have trolley buses and only the second to have electric lights in the street. By 1920 the boom was over and Manaus declined in importance. The legacy of the great wealth remains in the city in the form of the Teatro Amazonas Opera House built in 1896.

Manaus is the most frightening place I have every visited. In parts it seemed absolutely lawless. I felt I had landed in El Salvador in 1970. The port area was not safe after 8pm as a lot of the seamen carry guns! That, mixed with the locally brewed alcohol, created a situation I didn't need to be part of. Prostitutes were everywhere. I had travelled all this way into the centre of Brazil in search of the exotic, to find that with my red hair and green eyes I was the main attraction in town. I was clearly an outsider with dollars in my pocket, and for some, their meal ticket for the week.

Half of all televisions made in Brazil are fabricated in Manaus.

Teatro Amazonas

Manaus' famous opera house, the Teatro Amazonas, was designed in eclectic neoclassical style by engineers from Lisbon and a team of interior designers at the height of the rubber boom, and opened in 1896. More than any other building associated with the administration of Mayor Eduardo Ribeiro, this beautiful theatre symbolises the opulence that once was Manaus. The artists and most of the materials (Italian marble and glass, Scottish cast iron from Glasgow) were imported from Europe. The wood is Brazilian but even some of that was sent to Europe to be carved.

Built at the height of the city's wealth it stands as a symbol of culture imported from Europe to South America (in this case classical opera). The Opera House stars in the opening sequence of the Werner Herzog's epic film *Fitzcarraldo*.

One truly homespun feature was the roadway outside the opera house entrance, made of rubber so that late arriving carriages wouldn't create too much noise.

Although being 1,100km from the Atlantic, Manaus is only 60m above sea-level. This is quite amazing as it creates a landscape without landmarks or character. There are no mountain ranges or variations in climate, making the Amazonian region a relatively flat, very dense wilderness, with almost no roads and few pockets of population.

Two hours upstream from Manaus on the banks of the Rio Negro.

The water was very high as the river rises over ten metres from summer to winter. Many houses float to accommodate the change in water levels over the seasons.

When did we rename jungle as rainforest?
Are there technical (or cultural) differences between the two?
Jungle is a wild and hostile place, inhabited by fierce animals and deadly snakes, and populated by savage tribes of cannibals. These unfortunates live under the arbitrary tyranny of despotic chiefs and witch doctors, and are in desperate need of western medicine, white man's law, knowledge of the true gospel, and above all, civilisation, for which they are always grateful. This attitude, propagated by several Enlightenment philosophers (eg. Thomas Hobbes), is particularly strong in the modernist ethos of the first six decades of the 20th century, when it widely permeated both the sciences and the arts (see *Tarzan* movies).

Rainforest, on the other hand, is the location of benign, diverse and fragile nature, where many now endangered species coexist in harmony with tribes of gentle people living in a traditional, ecological manner, using an intricate knowledge of their local enivroment learned over many generationas, and stored, by them, as 'ancient wisdom' (see John Carpenter's *The Emerald Forest*). All contact between Western civilisation and such people is potentially dangerous, and should be discouraged.

Both images are stereotypes, the second harking back to Rousseau's Noble Savage, and the transcendentalists' (Emerson, Thoreau) concept of the value and importance of wilderness. The change to the use of rainforest probably took place sometime during the first wave of modern environmentalism, whose beginning many would date to the publication of Rachel Carson's *Silent Spring* (1962). Campaigns to save various bits of 'rainforest' found a receptive audience amoung the 'ecology' movement of the late 60s and early 70s.

Incidentally, careful reading of Rudyard Kipling's poem on this subject (in *The Jungle Book*) shows that the real law of the jungle (to act together) is the complete opposite of what most people think. A study recently published in *Nature* magazine suggests that democratic animal groups are much more coherent and successful than those that are run despotically.

— Dr Patrick O'Sullivan,
Environmental Science Department, University of Plymouth.
February 2003, *The Guardian*

//

USA:

Los Angeles → Death Valley → Las Vegas → Mojave Desert → Joshua Tree National Park ●

//

Los Angeles
On the attraction and mythologies of the West for immigrants:

They had also heard stories about the warm winter sunshine in California, the willing Mexican girls, mission wineries that never ran dry and vast uncountable herds of horses and cattle, ineptly guarded by docile Catholicised Indians — a fortune on the hoof that could be bought cheaply or easily stolen. California was already established in the American imagination as a mellow, easy-living golden land, with beautiful girls, a bountiful economy and plenty of suckers for the taking.

The average American lives in fourteen different houses during his or her lifetime.

Forget the Statue of Liberty.
The road is America's pre-eminent symbol of freedom.

In California there are generally many levels of access to what we call
the desert wilderness. So you have a lot of four-wheel drive roads for example,
where subscribers to the huge off-road vehicle culture go. These large
vehicles are a really good example of the breaking of the boundary between,
not necessarily the city, but urbanity or suburbia, and nature.

Nomad space: too far from the river to irrigate, too dry for crops or cities to take root. Like the deserts of the Bedouin, the Mongol steppes, the Tibetan plateaus or the buffalo plains, this is a harsh, marginal, wide-open landscape, with long horizons and a paucity of water.

'You have to get over the colour green.' wrote Wallace Stegner about the aethetics of Western landscape. 'You have to quit associating beauty with gardens and lawns; you have to get used to an inhuman scale'.

So try to think of Vegas this way: as America's Saturnalia, as the nonstop, year-round, 24-hour, American equivalent of that ancient Roman festival during which slaves took the roles of masters, only better and more glorious than that, since American slaves are less deeply afflicted by puritan values than their current masters.

… Or just think of it as our province of stupid dreams, but stupid dreams that tell true stories. Because desire (as Ferenczi was always reminding Freud) is a way of telling the truth, not knowing it — and Vegas tells the truth in ways that violate the canons and conventions of our culture's high and low with equal impunity.

Because people revel here who suffer at home — are free here who would otherwise languish in bondage. Bean-counters bet their kids' education on a roll of the dice. Kindergarten teachers gaze steely-eyed over the top of their cards, call your raise, and raise again. This is their secret place. From their hotel window, it stretches out into the night like a neon garden, supine in its worldly innocence, the pure virus of American culture denatured, literally, in the petri dish of the desert — virgin territory.

— Dave Hickey, 'Lost Boys', *Air Guitar: Essays on Art and Democracy*

… No, they're 747s and they all have these incredible interesting histories, but it's off limits now. It's a working airport, but it also acts as commercial airplane storage, along with hangars where F4s and decommissioned military planes owned by private citizens are stored. They also run a flight school where you can learn to fly military planes. It was shut down for a while because they were training people who were not American and when that came to light they closed it. I don't think you can get as much access to the airport now but you can't miss it and you can see a lot from the road. There are hundreds of jumbo jets lined up on the tarmac. If you have time it could be really interesting.

A lot of people go to Joshua Tree National Park for rock climbing. The other thing is to go out there with your dune buggy. On the weekend you'll see lots of people driving up the 5 (one of the main highways out of LA) with a couple of off-road vehicles and a trailer on the back, loaded with bikes. Motorcycle riding is really big. These are ways of experiencing nature that aren't necessarily considered traditional. You're not out there to look at the beautiful landscape, but more to drive through it and kick up some dust.

Southern California is a suburban environment. For most people visiting the desert is much more about recreation in nature rather than travelling through it or sightseeing. The idea of looking is alien to many people.

//

SCOTLAND:

Edinburgh →
Rannoch Moor ●

Scottish Parliament, Holyrood, Edinburgh

Designed by the late Spanish architect Enric Miralles, the new Scottish
Parliament building is seen by some commentators as a publicly
funded financial disaster, and by others as a symbol of Scotland's new
confidence and modern aspirations.

As is often the case with large public building projects, the construction has
had a troubled past. Originally proposed with a speculative budget of
£50 million, it is due to be formally opened by Queen Elizabeth II in October
2004, at a final cost of around £430 million.

At £8,922 per square metre it will be one of the most expensive
buildings in Britain.

The debating chamber will accommodate 219 public seats.

Palace of Holyroodhouse
At the foot of the Royal Mile, it has been described by some as the Queen's
northern Britain timeshare — she is here for a short time, during the summer
months, every year. Large parts of the palace are dull (Duke of Hamilton's Loo,
Queen's wardrobe) so only a dozen or so rooms are open to the public.

Scotland

Scotland, or in Gaelic, Alba, is a former kingdom located on the northern one third of the island of Great Britain. In 1707, the Kingdom of Scotland merged with the Kingdom of England to form the Kingdom of Great Britain (the King of Scotland had already inherited the English throne in 1603). In 1801 the Kingdom of Great Britain merged with the Kingdom of Ireland to form the United Kingdom of Great Britain and Ireland. In 1922, twenty-six of Ireland's thirty-two counties left the UK to form its own Irish Free State. Scotland remains part of the remaining kingdom, now known as the United Kingdom of Great Britain and Northern Ireland. In 1999, it received its own regional home rule parliament to govern Scotland on purely Scottish matters.

The West Highland Line
Source 3 — Lost on Rannoch Moor

This story, published in a magazine in 1927, gives an account of the ill-fated
journey of seven men who, on 30 January 1889, set out to survey a section
of Rannoch Moor on the proposed route for the West Highland Railway.
It shows just how wild and inhospitable the countryside was and how difficult
it must have been for the men who built the railway.

Lost on Rannoch Moor
A group of seven men — three civil engineers, two factors from local estates,
a lawyer representing the railway company and Robert McAlpine, the engineer
whose company built the second section of the line — planned to walk from
Spean Bridge to Rannoch Lodge, a distance of 72kms (45miles) to study the lie
of the land. They were not experienced walkers and set off without suitable
clothing and equipment.

Their journey proved to be disastrous from the start. The guide who was
supposed to accompany them along Loch Treig, just north west of Corrour,
failed to turn up as arranged. The weather then took a turn for the worse.
As they crossed the loch, they were caught in a sleet storm. Luckily they
found shelter at Lord Abinger's hunting lodge nearby but as staff did not know
to expect them, they spent a cold and hungry night there.

Next morning they decided to continue their survey and set off to cross
Rannoch Moor, an exposed and desolate place. The rain, wind, sleet and boggy
ground made progress slow. As daylight faded, matters worsened. The oldest
man in the group collapsed from fatigue. Two members of the group decided to
stay with him while the rest struggled on in the terrible weather to get help.
After some time, two members of the rescue group were forced to rest and take
shelter behind a large boulder. This left two members of the group, Robert
McAlpine and one of the engineers, James Bulloch, to find help. They decided
to split up and search in different directions.

Bulloch was the next casualty. He tripped over a fence in the dark and lay
unconscious in the open for four hours. When he regained consciousness, he
managed to follow the fence to a track, which eventually took him to Gortan,
north of Bridge of Orchy. There he alerted some local shepherds who set up a
search party to find his missing friends.

Luckily everyone in the group was rescued without serious injury. McAlpine
was found sheltering in a cottage three miles away from Gortan having
spent fourteen hours wandering the Moor by himself, soaking wet and covered
in mud. Had they been on the Moor the following day when a blizzard struck,
they might not have survived to tell the tale of their adventure.

The Moor of Rannoch is as wild and sombre a stretch of country as any in Scotland, especially when shrouded in mist or lashed by driving rain or snow, a terrifying wilderness for the lonely walker. In good weather, however, the Moor is a world of shining lochs with tree-clad islets and sandy bays, the way clothed with waving grass and purple heather, with unique views to delight the adventurous.

It covers some twenty square miles at a height of over 1,000 feet of peat and bog, for the most part laid on granite. It is the watershed of Central Scotland, where rivers start their journeys towards the Atlantic in the west and to the North Sea in the east. Over this area are scattered thousands of enormous rocks that have been torn from the sides of the hills and corries by a giant glacier moving eastwards 20,000 years ago.

'I see the land of Macbeth'

— Joseph Beuys, 1970

You can look at Rannoch Moor as a place of wonder, one of the last really wild places in Scotland. Or you can take Robert Louis Stevenson's view in the novel *Kidnapped*: 'A wearier looking desert a man never saw.'

He clearly caught it on a driech day.

Imagine a triangular area, stood on its apex, about ten miles across its base and about ten miles from top to bottom. Imagine that this fifty square mile inverted triangle is a roughly level plateau that sits at an altitude of a little over 1,000ft. Imagine that its surface is dotted with innumerable lochs, lochans, peat bogs, and streams; that it is surrounded by mountains that rise to over 3,000ft to the south-east and the west and to over 2,000ft in the north.

General site character:
Inland water bodies (standing water, running water) (10%)
Bogs. Marshes. Water fringed vegetation. Fens (72%)
Heath. Scrub. Maquis and garrigue. Phygrana (15%)
Dry grassland. Steppes (0.5%)
Humid grassland. Mesophile grassland (2%)
Inland rocks. Screes. Sands. Permanent snow and ice (0.5%)

Afterword

I had this idea about opposites, about urban space and wilderness.

I thought if I could get to the Amazon rainforest, it would help me understand Rio a little better, actually visiting Vegas (rather than just thinking about films set there), led me into this study of the areas in between places. Long straight roads are more fascinating than bright lights in the desert. Old places like Rannoch Moor being ruled by new democracies now feel really ancient. Open spaces in California becoming bike tracks, just to get by, still make me feel sad.

I love the concept of the frontier: the idea that there is always an edge to knowledge, that there are still things to learn. That bit on the map where there are no features, where we don't really know what happens, needs to be looked at again. It's widely argued that man has set foot on every place on earth, and that the wilderness no longer exists. I guess I agree, but it's personal. It's in your mind as much as in your feet.

Nathan Coley, August 2004

Published and distributed by **Book Works**
19 Holywell Row, London EC2A 4JB
www.bookworks.org.uk

ISBN 1 870699 67 X

Design: Practise
Print: Die Keure, Bruges

Book Works is funded by Arts Council England, and this publication has been
generously supported by the Scottish Arts Council

Thanks to the Scottish Arts Council for the support offered to Nathan Coley via
the Creative Scotland Awards, for the undertaking of research and travel which
has resulted in this book

1984–2004: Celebrating 20 years of Book Works

Rua Quintino Bocaiúva, 189 - 1º Andar - Sala 13
Manaus - Amazonas - Brazil - CEP: 69.005-110
Tel/Fax: 55-92-622-1246
e-mail: swallows@internext.com.br
web: www.swallowsandamazonstours.com

CITY OF LOS ANGELE
PARKING VIOLATION

CITATION # **930338253**

Date	Time Issued
11/13/02	01:48 PM

License Number	Time Marked
4WUL865	

State	Month	Year
CA	May	2003

VIN		
5802		

Vehicle Make	Type	Color
FORD	PAS	BLK

Location	Meter #/F
210 GRAND AV S	CC 1122

Officer	Serial No.
L. Jeciel	2327

Beat	Agency
621	56

IN VIOLATION OF SECTION: MC 88.13D
METER EXPIRED

AMOUNT DUE: **$35.00**

COMMENTS:
NO PLACARD VISIBLE   628849

Payment is required not later tha
calendar days from the date of
violation. You have 21 days to co
this citation.

SEE REVERSE SIDE FOR IMPORTANT INSTRUCTI

PAYMENT MUST BE IN U.S. FUND

* DO NOT SEND CASH *